Angels on High

Márton Váró's Limestone Angels on the
Nancy Lee and Perry R. Bass Performance Hall
in Fort Worth, Texas

For Mary Ann
'The Angel of Grand Rapids'
sculpture!

Bob Watson

Angels on High

Márton Váró's Limestone Angels on the
Nancy Lee and Perry R. Bass Performance Hall
in Fort Worth, Texas

Photographs by Rodger Mallison/*Fort Worth Star-Telegram*
Text by Ronald G. Watson
With Selections from Márton Váró's Photo Journal

TCU Press ▪ Fort Worth, Texas

Library of Congress Cataloging-in-Publication Data

Mallison, Rodger.

Angels on high : Márton Váró's limestone angels on the Nancy Lee and Perry R. Bass

Performance Hall in Fort Worth, Texas / photographs by Rodger Mallison :

text by Ronald G. Watson ; with selections from Márton Váró's photo journal.

Endsheet drawings/ Márton Váró

p> cm.

ISBN 0-87565-204-2 (hc. : alk. paper)

1. Váró, Márton. 2. Decoration and ornament, Architectural – Texas – Fort Worth.

3. Relief (Sculpture)—Texas—Fort Worth. 4. Angels in art. 5. Nancy Lee and Perry R. Bass

Performance Hall (Fort Worth, Tex.) I. Watson, Ronald G., 1941— . II. Title.

NB522.5.V38A4   1999

730'.92—dc21   99-21378

CIP

End sheet drawings by Márton Váró

Book and jacket design/ Margie Adkins Graphic Design

Angels on High is made possible by a gift from Ann and Malcolm Louden

In Honor Of

Mary D. and the late Howard F. Walsh, whose generous and loving hearts have made them true angels on whose wings others have soared.

CONTENTS

THE ANGELS IN THE CONTEXT OF PUBLIC SCULPTURE

Márton Váró's imposing angels emerge dramatically from the northern facade of the Nancy Lee and Perry R. Bass Performance Hall to herald the performing arts and to proclaim the Hall's purpose. In Bass Hall, Fort Worth has a building that is architecturally distinctive with monumental sculptures that are inseparable

East angel and City Center Tower.

from the building. These glorious beings are depicted at just the moment they are touching Earth, gliding on the last little bit of lift from their extended wings. Each angel hovers above the street, weightless and serene in flowing garments. Each one leans her torso, arms, and head slightly away from the background wall to play a golden trumpet high above. With a gesture that reinforces the trumpeting, each angel raises her other arm toward the sky. Since the Renaissance, classical winged figures with trumpets have been used to represent inspiration. These secular angels become the messengers who herald artistic productions and events in the Hall.

The sheer size of these serene figures strikes viewers before the more subtle aspects of the angel's symbolic charge can be understood. At approximately forty-eight feet tall the angels are several times larger than life. Like the Eiffel Tower in Paris or the Empire State Building in New York, Márton Váró's angels have quickly become symbols of Fort Worth as valid and commanding as the city's "cowtown" heritage. The angels are located on a city street, towering over the life beneath them. The decision to incorporate the building and the angels into the heart of the city, rather than set them apart by surrounding them with open space, was a deliberate and effective one. The size and scale of the angels in this urban corridor heightens the psychological quality of the site and forces viewers to concentrate on the building and its sculpture.

If it is well placed, public sculpture of imposing scale intensifies its site. For instance, Michaelangelo's placement of the free-standing equestrian portrait of Marcus Aurelius in the center of Campidolio in Rome and Jean-Bapiste Carpeaux's Dance relief on the façade of the Paris Opera House illustrate how sculpture and architecture can work together to define the aesthetic character of a site. The sculpture's placement, visibility and size enhance the site.

West angel.

Fourth Street in Fort Worth is strongly energized and lifted above its urban setting by the hovering presence of the angels.

By contrast a sculpture of a figure on a pedestal is an independent work of art, and its surroundings are of little importance. The pedestal frames it, and the "frame" sets it aside from the ordinary world.

Profiles.

Sculpture of this type might be placed outdoors but seldom bonds with the various other elements in the setting to become an effective public work because the "frame" of its pedestal works to separate it from anything and everything external to it. Although they are in a public location, such works remain essentially private. In addition to being impressive works of art, Márton Váró's angels bond with the architecture and the surrounding urban environment to create a complete aesthetic situation, the hallmark of successful public sculpture.

To fully experience the angels one must look beyond the walls that they spring from to the full three-dimensional context of the streetscape around them. The solid forms of the buildings around the angels and the spaces between these buildings result in varying impressions when the angels are viewed from different places in the street. The narrowness of the street in front of the angels compels viewers to see the angels from below and to always be closer to one. Thus, one angel always feels larger while the other is more remote and seems smaller. The sisters look exactly alike from only one vantage point directly across the street at the center of the Hall.

The angels' monumental scale and high visibility unite with the significant visual elements of Fourth Street to intensify this urban corridor and to concentrate viewers' attention on the building and its sculpture. Márton Váró's limestone angels clearly are effective public sculpture. Their intimate relationship to the Nancy Lee and Perry R. Bass Performing Arts Hall distinguishes them in the tradition of public sculpture. ▥

Maquette of west angel.

The Carving of the Angel Sculptures

From Márton Váró's point of view, this project began near the end of 1995 when he received a letter describing the new performance hall being designed for Fort Worth, Texas, by David Schwarz/ Architectural Services, Inc., of Washington, D.C. The design architect sent Váró a description of the project and a rendering of the building with a request for more information about his

The entry maquette.

sculpture. Schwarz was looking for a sculptor to create a monumental pair of symmetrical angels to embellish the new building. Within two months the sculptor met with Schwarz and Vicki Dickerson, the project manager, in Fort Worth to see the site and a larger rendering of the proposed building.

This meeting began a dialogue between the entire design team and the sculptor. They agreed that the sculptor was free to create his conception of angels that would harmonize with the architecture. He was not expected to carve the architect's design. In other words, this was to be a creative sculptural project in collaboration with the design team similar to the collaboration between the engineer Gustave Eiffel and the sculptor Auguste Bartholdi when they built the Statue of Liberty. As a result of this interview Váró carved a single angel in limestone at his California studio. This angel became his entry maquette in the ensuing competition. This exactingly detailed maquette communicated Varo's vision of the whole project. In fact, the small maquette (or model) is a completely realized sculptural work that accurately foreshadowed the feeling of the final angels. Although the completed sculptures differ somewhat from the artist's first proposal, their solemn dignity and serenity were determined at the inception of the sculptural project.

The competition to select the sculptor was conducted in two phases. The first phase required competing artists to create figures of angels as they visualized them for the building and the site. Schwarz and

Márton Váró at work on the east angel in California. The maquette of the angel he is carving is at the right of the picture.

In California the sculptor refines the drapery of the east angel.

Dickerson reviewed each submission and determined that additional conditions would need to be fulfilled before they would select the sculptor to receive the commission. In Váró's case, they recommended more restrained activity in the figure and a diminution of the illusion of her emergence from the facade. The sculptor thought long and hard about these recommendations and reviewed the project's architectural elements before he agreed to alter his initial design. Although they had wanted an art deco style for the sculptures, the architects did not insist on this requirement because they wanted original sculpture, not just skillful eclecticism.

Actually, because Váró and the design team were mainly in harmony, only a few mutually agreed concessions from both sides were necessary to forge a sound working relationship between the principals and to form a like-minded creative design team devoted to the successful completion of the angels.

The sculptor carving the wings, on the ground in Fort Worth.

This concord between Váró and the design team led him into the second phase of the competition that required a larger maquette from each competing sculptor. Márton Váró's four-foot maquette convinced the design team of his ability to execute the required work creatively. He was awarded the contract and immediately began working on what he called "the commission of a lifetime."

These figures are the largest angels ever carved in high relief. However, the artist says that the importance of the project lies not in size but in the angels being an integral part of the building and with the building becoming an important landmark in downtown Fort Worth.

Márton Váró shields his face from a stream of limestone dust as he uses an angle grinder with a diamond blade to make a deep cut in the wings.

The artist does not dismiss as unimportant the enormous size of these figures. In fact, after he received the commission he was in Carrara, Italy, where the quarries Michelangelo used are located. Stone carvers from all over the world come to this part of Italy to work and to consult the resident experts on technical (and sometimes aesthetic) matters related to their work. Váró had the opportunity to discuss his commission at great length with Carlo Nicoli, owner of a firm that provides architectural marble worldwide and does architectural carvings on commission. Nicoli said that he did not think one man working alone could bear up under the challenge of keeping the figures straight, upright, and symmetrical. Váró was willing to take the risk. He has said that, "I was at a point in my career when I was ready to carve a very large work when these angels appeared."

His first responsibility as the commissioned artist was to meet with the people of Linbeck Construction Corporation and Justin Industries/Texas Quarries Division at the quarry in Cedar Park, near Austin, Texas, where the stone would be quarried for the sculpture. He asked to see the layers of the stone formation and to have a sample of its consistency because Texas limestone was a material new to him and he needed to learn its characteristics. He visited the quarry site and saw the conditions surrounding the deposit of stone that the architects had selected for the building's cladding and for the sculpture. The vein of stone was seven to nine feet deep, just below the earth's surface. The quarrying process required that the surface dirt be removed, the stone cut and removed, and the resulting cavity filled before moving on. The quarry is a flat expanse of open land that facilitates this process. Many quarries are much more complicated to work; this is what the sculptor called, "a lucky situation." He said that, "the limestone is soft, nice to carve and it has a warm color."

The company shipped the quarried stone to Váró's studio in California where he carved two symmetrical angels at a proportion of one sixth of the completed project's full scale. From these angels (the third maquette Váró created to visualize the project) engineers at Curtain Wall Design & Consulting, Inc. (CDC, Inc.) were able to calculate the exact dimensions needed for each block designed by the artist, and they were able to design lifting devices for each one. Their work was so well executed that when the blocks were lifted they were stable, horizontally exact and ready to be set on the wall. Váró spent many productive hours on the phone with Lloyd Breaux of CDC, Inc., collaborating on the design of the blocks and various aspects of their permanent installation.

In California, with the help of University of California/Irvine welders, Márton Váró devised a rack to support the blocks of stone and a method to secure three courses of stone at one time. These inventions allowed him to keep all aspects of the figures under control as he carved the individual blocks. They also proved to be important safety features: there were no accidents, and there was no damage, not even chipping, to the stone blocks. The holding rack allowed him to carve the figures from the lowest register to the highest in successive rows of stone blocks. Both figures were carved at the same time, with Váró carving parallel sections of each angel simultaneously. The sculptor began at the foot and progressed up to the head of each angel. His process was systematic: when he finished carving the first three courses he numbered each block, removed the lower two courses, and stored the blocks for shipment to Fort Worth. The upper course of blocks then became the lowest after he placed the next two courses of uncarved blocks on top of it. This method allowed Váró to align the uncarved blocks with those immediately below them. He repeated this method all the way through the carving process. Although the height of the sculptures

The sculptor carves a limestone block to form one of the angel's sleeves.

precluded him from seeing them assembled until they were installed in Fort Worth, the accuracy of his maquettes and of the engineering drawings provided him adequate information for his carving. This part of the work was conducted on the campus of the University of California, Irvine. The maintenance workshop staff was accommodating when it was necessary to move and to load the stone blocks. They provided whatever the artist needed including ladders, a forklift, and carpenters during the year-and-a half that it took for Váró to carve the angels. FAE Worldwide shipped all of the carved blocks from California to Fort Worth. Their expert care resulted in a perfect shipment with no damage to any of the stone blocks.

Although much of each figure was completed in California, the major blocks for the arms were carved at the quarry in Cedar Park, Texas. Váró worked there on the large blocks after completing the other sections in California. The largest and heaviest blocks in the figures are the upper arms that project perpendicularly from each angel. Each upper arm is made of one piece of stone eight feet long weighing eight

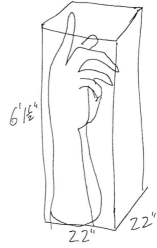

Drawing/Márton Váró

tons. Attached to each of these sections is a forearm that leads to the wrist supporting the trumpet. These pieces representing the forearm are about eight feet long and weigh three tons each. Váró carved them in California, but the size and weight of the upper arm blocks necessitated carving them closer to the Fort Worth site. Váró said, "I had a taste of Texas' beautiful spring weather at the Justin Featherlite Sawmill while I carved the blocks for the arms. We also experienced a killer tornado that passed within 300 yards of the work site!" The *Austin American-Statesman* reported that "Tornadoes cut a deadly swath through Central Texas on May 27, 1997 leaving at least 31 dead in Jarrell in Williamson County, collapsing a grocery store roof in Cedar Park, and causing at least two deaths in Travis County." This store was Váró's favorite; he shopped there every evening. Fortunately, there was no damage, and no one was injured at the sculpture site. With gratitude, the artist said, "We were protected by angels."

The sculptor refines the arm of the west angel in place on the Performance Hall facade.

In June of 1997 Márton Váró came to the construction site in Fort Worth to carve the wings. There are some twenty blocks in the wings and the delicacy of them required more carving time than the artist had anticipated. As summer wore on the temperatures passed the hundred-degree mark. Váró said that, "I noticed that there were multiple shadows cast on the work, and I realized that light reflected from the neighboring high-rise buildings was creating a solar furnace for me." He finished the first set of wings and then returned to California to carve the hands, noting that "it was refreshing to be in California in August." On September 8th he returned to Fort Worth to carve the second set of wings, to consult with the technicians who were installing all the blocks and to supervise the installation of the whole sculptural project.

Váró credits Linbeck engineer Chris Davis for managing the project with great skill and finesse. During the installation, a crew of Linbeck ironworkers and stonemasons paralleled Váró's carving process by setting the lowest course of blocks in place first and then by positioning the remaining blocks in order. The last set on the façade were the highest blocks of the wings that completed each angel. Although the installation was trouble free, there were minor adjustments needed at every step. Váró and the crew were anxious throughout the process because the enormous size of the sculptures made a full-scale test unfeasible. The angels were not assembled anywhere except on the facade of Bass Hall. Everyone involved thought that the carving and the engineering were accurate, but no one knew for certain until the blocks were in place. This condition also meant that the artist and the public saw the complete figures at the same time. As soon as all the blocks were set Váró worked to heighten the continuity of the forms before the scaffolding was removed for the Hall's grand opening. Thus, years of solitary carving in a remote and quiet outdoor setting in California culminated in the most protracted public performance of the artist's career while he rapidly made countless refinements throughout each figure. ▪

Selections from Márton Váró's Photo Journal

These photos record the very beginning of the carving process. After visiting the quarry to study the limestone, the artist spent almost a year carving the maquettes, designing the blocks, and devising a method to use in carving the full-size angels before he began work on the final figures.

Márton Váró took photographs to study his work as it progressed. He said about them, "At night I would look at these photos of the day's work and because they were two dimensional I could almost see the work as if I did not carve it. Looking at the photos I saw errors that I could not see when I was carving. I suppose that I would repeat a mistake so many times in a day's work that I thought it was correct."

Váró had no assistants in the actual carving process. He said, "I wanted to have the sole responsibility for the outcome of the carving; no other hand should be visible in my work. If it comes out badly or flawed in some way, I am responsible. I will have no one to blame".

Váró and the design team controlled the proportions of the sculptures by dividing the figures into nineteen layers or courses using a standard construction module for stone cladding on large buildings. Each course is almost thirty-two inches high and each block is separated from the one above and the one below by a three-eighths inch space for mortar. The maquettes were similarly divided into five-inch courses: therefore, every dimension of the full-size sculpture is six times larger than the corresponding one in the maquette. Every block of each angel was numbered beginning with the lowest ones. ▪

The sculptor visiting the quarry in Texas.

The first eight massive blocks of the east angel on the carving rack form a stone "pyramid." The easel at the left holds the corresponding eight blocks of the maquette that guided the artist's carving of the full-scale figure.

The artist with the partially carved lowest blocks of the east angel. To the right is the model of the façade constructed at one-sixth the size of the actual building.

Photo: Bill Gorajia

This photograph, showing blocks 9, 10, and 11 of each angel on the carving rack, demonstrates the sculptor's method of carving from the lower blocks up to the upper ones. Throughout the carving process, as blocks were removed from the carving rack, Fine Arts Express packed the finished blocks and shipped them to Fort Worth. This photograph reveals that the first eight blocks have been removed.

The eastern angel on the left is a clear example of the way the sculptor removed finished blocks but always retained one to guide him in the transition to the two new ones above. The lowest block (#9) is carved to a high state of completion. Váró has drawn lines on the block above to guide him in carving the flow of the drapery. The sculptor stood on the cubic boxes in front of the blocks during carving sessions.

It is the sculptor's task to reveal the figure in the block by removing all the stone that hides it from us; therefore, he must be conscious of both the surface of the figure and of its form beneath the surface. There is an internal structure and an external structure in a fully conceived and realized figurative sculpture. Study of these photographs reveals the relatively simple, flat planar forms the sculptor began with in order to achieve the smooth, highly developed cascading drapery that will seem taut over the slightly bent knee of each finished figure. This drapery unites all the major features of the lower extremities and the torso into one simple yet lissome form. If the sculptor did not have a strong vision of the internal structure of the human figure, these surface refinements would not produce the vibrancy of the body that the convincing and expressive sculpture possesses.

Márton Váró in a pose similar to that of the eastern angel. Note the folds radiating across the top block (#18) and wrapping around the form. The contrast of the multiple folds against the smoothness of the figure's opposite side animates and intensifies the sculpture.

The figures are not identical or mirror images of each other. Although both figures balance by sustaining their weight on one leg and steady their balance with the other, the way the drapery gathers and falls significantly differs in these corresponding versions of block #18. In fact, the corresponding folds and clinging fabric on the supporting leg of each figure originate from different points on the figures and take different downward paths.

The board of the easel that Váró used to support the maquette blocks as a reference and guide to carve the full-scale blocks. In this photograph blocks #21, #24, and #29 are in place. Although this is a simple device fabricated of plywood lumber, it is a critical tool in the carver's process. The holes drilled in the board receive pins that project from each block's back. The pins are made of threaded rod stock, and each one is secured to the plywood with a wing nut. These pins support each block; no weight is transferred from the higher blocks to the lower ones. Thus, the maquette imitates the installation of the full-scale blocks on the actual building where each block is welded to a steel structural element of the building. The weight of each block is transferred to the building; not to the lower blocks.

The figures at the midway point of the project (block #21 is in the tenth course of nineteen courses).

For the first time the projection of the angels away from the wall can be seen and felt. The pipe jacks in this picture are simple and expedient tools. Although they seem so small, they add to the sculptor's safety and support the massive stones. The blocks were also welded to the rack with one-inch diameter rods that were embedded two feet into each stone block.

The rubble in front of the performance hall's mock façade and the full-scale torsos on the carving rack. This view shows the amount of stone that had to be removed to reveal the angels.

This view of the torso of the eastern angel shows the intricate folding of the drapery. The flat faces of blocks #24 and #29 create the opening that will receive the massive block #25, which represents the raised arm holding the trumpet. Block #25 must also have a corresponding flat, perpendicular surface that slides up against these two blocks; yet these two blocks cohere in such a way that they appear to be the internal structure of the angel's body.

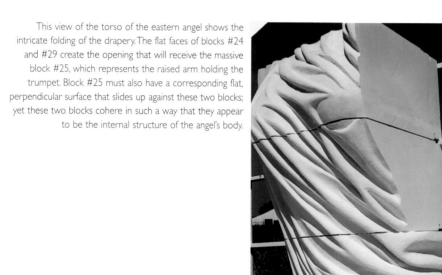

The full-size torso of the eastern angel is depicted alongside the maquette with the raised arm (block #25) in place.

The sculptor standing with both blocks numbered #33.

Márton Váró is carving the face of the western angel. The massive block to the right of the face (#32) was needed for the drapery of the angel's uplifted left arm.

The western angel's wing feathers, part of block #33, are roughed in behind her head. This photo illustrates the extreme high relief of the upper torso, arms and head of these sculptures.

Near the project's completion Márton Váró posed with his friend, the attorney Kenneth Kleinberg, who quipped that he represented the angels.

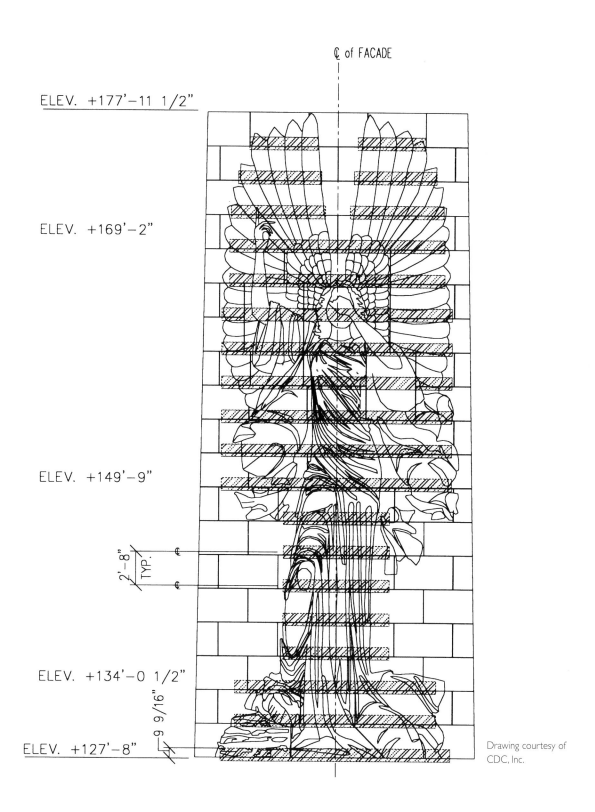

℄ of FACADE

ELEV. +177'−11 1/2"

ELEV. +169'−2"

ELEV. +149'−9"

2'−8"
TYP.

ELEV. +134'−0 1/2"

9 9/16"

ELEV. +127'−8"

Drawing courtesy of
CDC, Inc.

Rodger Mallison's Photographs

Rodger Mallison is a senior photographer for the *Fort Worth Star-Telegram*, with a special interest in architectural photography. He covered the construction of Bass Hall for the *Star-Telegram* for over two years, from the time the first steel trusses spanning the auditorium were lifted into place to the first performances. A native of Dallas, Mallison has been with the newspaper for twenty-two years and has thirty years photographic experience. ▪

Váró watches the placement of the first block.

A stonemason setting one of the stainless steel lifting devices

Márton Váró

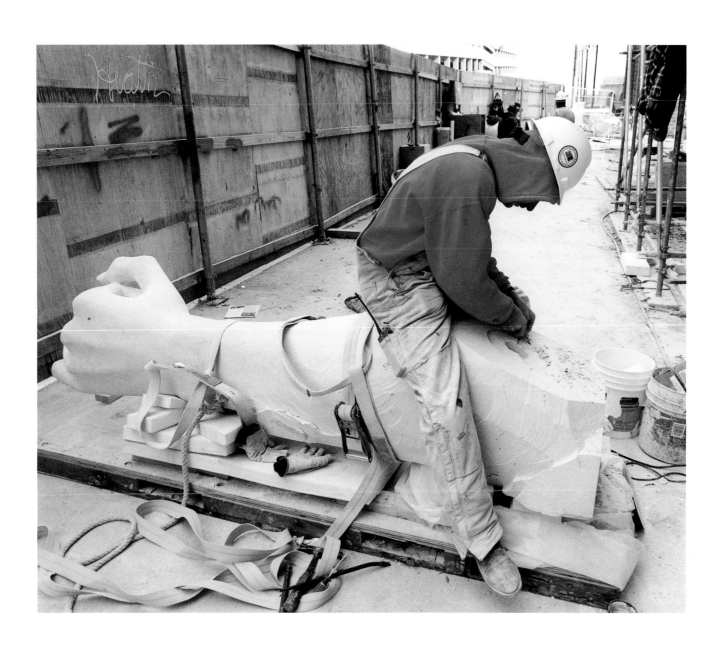

Márton Váró

Martón Váró

Born in Székelyudvarhely, Transylvania, Hungary (now Romania) in 1943, Márton Váró was educated at the Ion Andreescu School of Fine Arts in Cluj, Romania. He has held a Dekovits Fellowship and a Fulbright Scholarship at the University of California in Irvine, attended various seminars and working tours in Europe and America, and served as artist-in-residence in Brea, California. He currently makes his home in Irvine.

Váró has had solo exhibitions in Germany, Hungary, and Romania, and his work has been included in group exhibitions in Italy, Canada, Finland, Sweden, Spain, the USSR, France, Belgium, Holland, Romania and the United States. It appears in collections in museums, galleries, and public buildings in several countries, including the United States, and may be seen as close to Fort Worth as the Plaza of the Americas in Dallas.

His awards include the Medgyessy Medal of the City of Debrecen and that of the Studio of Young Artists, the Munkácsy Prize, and an award from the Ladányi Foundation in New York.

A catalog of Váró's work is available from Vario Studio, 2 Charity, Irvine, California 92612.

Selected Public Collections

Pereira Sculpture Garden
UCI, California

Plaza of the Americas
Dallas, Texas

Peace Memorial
Palm Desert, California

City of Brea, California

City of Volos, Greece

County Administration Building
Debrecen, Hungary

Kálvin Plaza
Debrecen, Hungary

Berettyóújifalu City Hall
Debrecen, Hungary

Convention Center
Budapest, Hungary

Forum Hotel
Budapest, Hungary

City of Burgas, Bulgaria

Debrecen, Hungary

Debrecen Clock Tower, Hungary

Szombathely City Hall, Hungary

Debrecen New Post Office
Debrecen, Hungary

Mátészalka Textile Factory (BFK)

Berettyóújifalu Elzett Works
Hungary

City Sculpture Garden
Prilep Macedonia, Yugoslavia

Central Finland Museum of Art
Jyvaskyla, Finland

Stedelijk Museum
Amsterdam, Holland

Ministry of Culture
Collection at the Exhibition Hall
Budapest, Hungary

National Gallery
Budapest, Hungary

Móra Ferenc Museum
Szeged, Hungary

Deri Museum
Debrecen, Hungary

Dr. Petru
Groza City, Romania

Muzeul Tarii Crisurilor
Oradea, Romania

Acknowledgements

During a dinner in Fort Worth before the angels were completely installed Márton Váró and I were discussing the project. In response to my question about who was documenting his work, he told me that Rodger Mallison had been photographing it for the *Fort Worth Star-Telegram* almost from the inception of the commission but that no one was writing about it. This book began during that conversation.

I soon learned that Rodger had some 4,000 negatives and that Márton had several hundred snapshots. In addition to these visual resources, Terrell Lamb gave me helpful information on the design team and their processes that allowed me to formulate a proposal to the TCU Press to publish this record of a unique public-art project. I am grateful for the enthusiastic response of Dr. Larry Adams, TCU associate provost for academic affairs, and for the expertise and good will of Dr. Judy Alter, director of the TCU Press.

A major contribution in the form of a publication subvention from Ann and Malcolm Louden turned my mental images into an actual book. I thank everyone who understood the importance of publishing a record of this project.

Rodger Mallison was an extremely patient guide to his photographic archive. He deserves credit for reducing the pool of images to about 250 arresting photographs. From them I selected the illustrations for the book. He also worked closely with Margie Adkins West on the color separations of the final photographs. Margie's excellent design captures the drama of the finished sculptures and her layout of the book forcefully builds from the sculptor's first visit in the quarry to the intensity of the opening festivities and light show that was part of the dedication of Bass Hall.

Márton Váró advised me on all matters of fact, time and place. I appreciate his forthrightness about his work; his candor made this book possible. Although he carved the angels by himself, architects, engineers, stone masons, ironworkers, and others were indispensable. Many of them are pictured in this book and I would like to commend everyone who helped to realize the angels. Various people from Performing Arts Fort Worth were helpful in providing information and interest throughout the project.

Thanks to Judy Alter for her sharp eyes and quick mind as the editor of my manuscript. I am indebted to Lynda Lesher for her constant support as I wrote. Her proofreading was invaluable, but any errors are mine alone.

Ronald Watson
Fort Worth, Texas 1999